Step by Step
Home Buying Guide

A how-to-guide for saving time and money, when buying your home.

By Wyn Ray

Library of Congress Registration Number: TXu002187771

ISBN: 978-0-9960018-5-4 (Printed Book)

First Printing: 2020

NOTE TO READERS

Step by Step Home Buying Guide contains the opinions and ideas of its author Wyn Ray and ASKWYNHOW.COM, LLC. It is intended to provide helpful and informative material for most residential property. The strategies outlined in this guide may not be suitable for every individual and are not guaranteed or warranted to produce any results because every situation, house or property is uniquely different. Any names used in this guide have been changed.

Step by Step Home Buying Guide is sold with the understanding that Wyn Ray or ASKWYNHOW.COM, LLC are not rendering legal, financial, accounting, or other professional advice or services. The reader understands that Wyn Ray is a licensed real estate broker only in the state of Minnesota, #20399255. You may choose to consult a competent professional before adopting any of these suggestions in this "how to guide" book or drawing inferences from it.

The reader acknowledges that **Step by Step Home Buying Guide** may not be perfectly

The reader understands that a portion of the profits from this guide will cause *a donation* to non-profit organizations who *provide housing*, or who *provide clean water* by renewing or building wells in Africa or who *provide food* such as "Feed My Starving Children."

Thank you, Cliff Johnson, for all your editing suggestions and your valuable time spent helping this book become a reality.

All photos used for the cover and back cover were purchased from onepony/iStock/Thinkstock by Getty Images.

Thank you, Angela Rambo, for finalizing the front and back book cover.

"We Create Success Together!"

Contents

Forward

Forward

The story behind "Step by Step Home Buying Guide."

After my daughter Jessica got her real estate license, I became motivated to write *"Step by Step Home Buying Guide"*. It was my best advice for her as she was about to launch her real estate sales career. My other daughter Tessa decided to purchase her first home. I wanted Tessa to have a guide to better help her know the right steps for how to buy her first home.

This book has a sequence of steps, suggestions, and checklists that you may choose to follow when you buy your home. This book will serve you well!

After I graduated from college, I taught elementary and middle school for four years. In 1980, after having taught children for three years, I obtained a Minnesota Real Estate Salespersons license. In 1980 the interest rates for home mortgages were beginning to climb to historical highs and October 1981 they peaked at 18.45%! This adversity helped me become a better real estate agent.

Early in my career I was extremely comfortable teaching first-time homebuyer seminars and I also created a "packet" of information that I could review with someone who could not attend the seminar. I received incredibly positive feedback from the seminars and one-on-one meetings in which I covered the steps for successfully buying a home. Some of the information in my original "packet" is found in this book.

I have helped many homebuyers successfully purchase homes and after becoming Broker, I have had the pleasure of training hundreds of real estate agents on how to help homebuyers have a pleasant home buying experience.

My motto is "We Create Success Together!"

CHAPTER ONE

Why do you want to own a home?

Home ownership is the American dream!

I have asked many buyers this question and the most typical reasons they give are:

- Having more privacy.
- Having control over décor.
- Paying down the principal for you versus a landlord.
- Having an asset after paying off the mortgage.
- Tax deduction from interest and property taxes.
- No capital gains after owning for 2 years.
- Owning something that is your own.
- Having pets without approval from a landlord.
- Having a yard for children to play in.

- Amenities such as fireplace, craft room or having a garden.

- Living near community amenities such as parks, schools, nature preserves, bus lines, shopping, and lakes for example.

- Hosting family holidays and backyard BBQ's.

- It is the American dream to own a home.

I suggest that you take the time to list the top three reasons why you want to own a home.

Answering the following questions will help guide professionals who may help you successfully find your dream home.

What is your goal?

What is your deadline?

How will it matter?

What do you want to have happen?

What do you not want to have happen?

CHAPTER TWO

Real Estate Companies are not equal.

Real estate companies are not a commodity.

There are many benefits to working with an agent who is part of a large company. Typically, large companies have more resources for buyers and many offer one-stop-shopping. They may offer in-house mortgage financing; title services, a home protection plan, homeowners' insurance, and some have concierge services. Studies have shown that upwards of 65% to 75% of homebuyers like one-stop-shopping.

A small company or broker may include similar services as the larger real estate companies. There are some excellent smaller "boutique" real estate companies who represent many buyer transactions in specific communities or neighborhoods.

The real estate broker supervises the activities of its salespeople. The broker provides education, training, support systems, technology, and a culture to work in. Some agents are well educated, and some are not.

It is good to know how long a real estate company has been in business. Stability with the future in mind is worth considering. Will they be around in the future when you want to sell your home? Do they store your documents electronically, or enabling you to have access to them in the future?

Many homebuyers choose a real estate company based on reputation, ethics, trustworthiness, and stewardship in the communities it serves.

CHAPTER THREE
Selecting the Right Agent

Finding an agent who has your best interest at heart is what you are looking for.

Agent selection – new agent

I have been a broker and manager of real estate offices and I have witnessed many new agents who have successfully completed their first real estate transaction for a homebuyer.

Most of the time it is a friend or relative who the homebuyer has known for a while. They want to help the new agent get off to a successful start in their career. The new agent and homebuyer have the benefit of using me a resource for the entire transaction. Who is their broker or mentor?

Most who choose to work with a new agent decide they really like and trust them. New agents may also have the latest and greatest real estate sales training and have lots of time to devote to a homebuyer.

Some designations newer agents may have:

- The Realtor® designation is a trademarked designation given to members of the National Association of Realtors®. Agents have completed and agree to abide by a Code of Ethics.

- A GRI designation GRADUATE, REALTOR® INSTITUTE represents an extensive training program sponsored by a State Association.

Agent selection – experienced agent

After working in the real estate industry for over 40 years, I may be prejudiced but I would attest to the benefits of working with a successful and experienced agent who has at least five years' experience.

There are several designations that experienced real estate agents may earn. Here are some of the many designations that I have earned, and which may be important to you in selecting an agent:

- A CRS designation, CERTIFIED RESIDENTIAL SPECIALIST is a National Association of Realtors® designation requiring documentation of necessary coursework completion, a verified number of transactions completed and number of years with experience.

- An ABR designation, ACCREDITED BUYER REPRESENTATIVE is a National Association of Realtors® designation given to Realtors® who have completed an advanced course focused on representing homebuyers.

- An ePro designation represents a designation awarded by the National Association of Realtors® for completing a technology certification program.

I have many friends who are awesome real estate agents who do not have many designations.

I believe that real estate agents who have earned designations are usually dedicated to learning more about their profession and I believe that will benefit you as a homebuyer.

Interviewing an Agent

When you meet with a real estate agent, in addition to their experiences and successes there are several important topics to discuss. I have found that most homebuyers look to a real estate agent for the following:

- Help with determining affordability

- Help finding the right home

- Pricing and negotiations

- Help with the paperwork

I wrote this book to reflect what I cover with someone who meets with me to discuss working together. I have found that everyone has different levels of experience or knowledge and there is no need to discuss something that is not of concern.

Many first-time buyers will tell me that they would like to cover all the topics and confess that they do not know what they are supposed to ask. The next page is a questionnaire that I created for you to use when meeting with a real estate agent.

What is important to you in the purchase of your new home?

Please rank the following topics from 1 to 5, with 1 being not concerned to 5 being of most concern to you.

Broker and agent qualifications

Agency representation

Finding the right home

Current market statistics

Help with determining affordability

Understanding the home-buying process

Help with the paperwork

Communication

Negotiation strategy

Offer presentation

Having a home inspection

Buyer services guarantee

Financing options and guarantees

Neighborhood and/or schools

Having a home warranty

Post purchase follow up

Web based access to your documents

How does your agent get paid for representation?

The following chapters will address many of the topics found in the previous questionnaire.

After gaining information from your questions, reviewing the real estate agent's experience, designations, and other offerings, it is time to sign an Exclusive Right to Represent Contract.

The Contract will have a start and end date. How the broker will be compensated with commission will be spelled out, including any fixed broker commission.

It is important to have a written contract that specifies your broker and agent's responsibilities along with your responsibilities.

Every state is different; however, the fundamental fiduciary duties of a real estate agent are:

Loyalty – broker/salesperson will act only in client(s)' best interest.

Obedience – broker/salesperson will carry out all client(s)' lawful instructions.

Disclosure – broker/salesperson will disclose to clients(s)' all material facts of which broker/salesperson has knowledge which might reasonably affect the client(s)' use and enjoyment of the property.

Confidentiality – broker/salesperson will keep clients(s)' confidences unless required by law to disclose specific information (such as disclosure of material facts to Buyers).

Reasonable Care – broker/salesperson will use reasonable care in performing duties as an agent.

Accounting – broker/salesperson will account to client(s) for all client(s)' money and property received as agent.

Your responsibilities include:

Exchange necessary information for how you like to be communicated with. In person, by phone, texting, email or use of a social media tool. Also, communicating any new information regarding your homebuying situation.

Barriers to a successful home buying experience:

- Lack of information. (See the previous questionnaire.)
- Knowing current market data and trends
- Having unrealistic expectations
- Afraid to make a mistake
- Getting ahead of the process
- Bad advice from non-professionals
- Who is on your real estate agent's team to help you? A real estate team may include a loan officer, title closer, home inspector and other service providers that your real estate agent has found trustworthy.

CHAPTER FOUR

Get Approved for a Mortgage

It is in your best interests to get pre-approved for a mortgage before you seriously look at homes.

Most folks are curious as to what they can afford for a mortgage payment and what amount they are able to borrow. Most buyers want help with *determining affordability*.

There are five components to getting a mortgage underwriter's final approval for your loan. They are:

1) Acceptable credit score.
2) Verified employment of at least two years.
3) Verified money for the purchase.
4) Satisfactory appraisal for the home and price.
5) Acceptable title work for the home.

A mortgage approval with an underwriter requires verification of your credit score, employment with acceptable income and available money to purchase.

With partial verifications of the first three components a loan officer will issue a pre-approval letter which helps validates your offer to purchase. A pre-approval letter simply assures a Seller and their listing agent, that some due diligence has been completed by the loan officer and their underwriter. There are disadvantages of a pre-qualification letter versus the advantages of a pre-approval letter.

Disadvantages of a pre-qualification letter

Most *"pre-qualified"* lender letters are generated by loan officers with unverified information, simply after a conversation between the borrower and loan officer.

Experienced real estate agents will advise their sellers to not sign a purchase agreement with a buyer who presents a pre-qualification letter with their offer to purchase. Often, the mortgage will not be approved because the original information discussed was not correct. Credit reports with lower scores, a recent bankruptcy, a forgotten debt, excessive student loans or insufficient funds to purchase are several real-world examples.

Even if you know that your credit, employment, and funds to purchase are good, the pre-qualification letter is not what you want to present to a seller with your offer to purchase.

The advantages of a pre-approval letter

The most critical advantage of being pre-approved for your mortgage is the potential to save several thousand dollars in negotiating a lower price with a seller. Being pre-approved for a mortgage is almost like having a cash offer.

Another advantage that I have witnessed is when homebuyers are in a competitive offer situation with another buyer or several buyers for the same home. The homebuyer who has a pre-approved loan often beats out the other buyer or buyers because the losing offer(s) only could present a pre-qualification letter which is close but not good enough. Some sellers have taken a lower offer over a higher priced offer because the buyer with the lower offer had a mortgage pre-approval letter. This saves time from looking at more homes, which may not be as nice as the original home lost to another buyer.

I consider time to be of value and therefore saving time is like saving money.

Methods for getting a mortgage pre-approval

There are several ways to get pre-approved for a mortgage. Typically, you give a loan officer your social security number so they may order your credit report. They also verify your income with pay stubs, get copies of your bank statements and then submit an online application for your loan pre-approval. The computer software will respond with a pre-approval and maximum amount of monthly payment. This is commonly called **pre-*approval with laptop underwriting***.

If you are self-employed or have commissions as part of your income, it may take two weeks for getting a mortgage pre-approval. Applicants will need to provide the last two years of filed tax returns. This pre-approval process involves submitting the documentation to an underwriter who reviews the file to make sure that an investor will buy the mortgage. **Mortgage origination companies do not typically want to hold or own your mortgage.** There is an extensive checklist for verification required by the investor who will fund the mortgage. The quote, *"He who has the gold makes the rules"* still rings true today.

Several buyers have told me that they did not want to overspend and buy what they were pre-approved for. Really great loan officers and real estate agents work within the parameters that buyers set with regards to a monthly payment and corresponding mortgage amount. After looking at options many

buyers have told me to raise the price range of homes because they were not finding what they wanted. Only you the homebuyer will make this decision.

What is a gift letter?

Over half of first-time homebuyers get some down payment assistance from a relative. The lender needs to obtain a document known as a gift letter. The gift letter is a form that must be signed by the relative with the source of their money being verified. Most relatives are surprised that their act of kindness requires a verification of their bank account as proof of where they got the funds from. If you need to ask a relative for a gift, I always recommend inviting them out for dinner.

Proof of sale required

If you need to sell your house to have a down payment to purchase your next home, then you will need to provide a copy of a net proceeds or HUD-1 statement to the underwriter who is approving the mortgage for purchasing your next home. They want proof that you have paid off the other mortgage.

CHAPTER FIVE
Know What Your Costs Will Be

Homebuyers have a legal right to know what their estimated closing costs and monthly payment are before signing a purchase agreement.

Early in my real estate career I purchased a car and was surprised by some last-minute expenses. I vowed that I would not put homebuyers through the same experience.

Closing costs are expenses that a lender charges to complete the loan and get the money to the closing table. Closing costs can be estimated when you meet with the loan officer and get your approval started. This is valuable information to know before you start looking at homes. It is good to know how much money you will need to purchase your home before you sign a binding contract with a seller.

I am not a loan officer, but I know that an estimate of closing costs or what was commonly known as a good faith estimate is required to be provided to homebuyers. Some loan officers do not complete an estimate until a home is under contract between the buyer and seller.

A hypothetical estimate can be completed during the mortgage approval application. The obvious advantage is that you will know how much money is needed for your down payment and closing costs. This amount is known as your acquisition cost to purchase a home.

Many loan programs require the buyer to have a **minimum acquisition cost**. This restricts a seller's contribution towards the buyer's closing costs. For example, if your minimum acquisition cost is $8,900.00, the seller cannot contribute any money to reduce that amount. The investor wants the buyer to have a difficult time walking away from that much money.

All lenders are required to determine a buyer's **Ability-to-Repay** along with a **Debt-to-Income ratio test.** The current FHA debt-to-income ratio is 43%. FHA has determined that a borrower's monthly debt does not exceed 43% of the borrower's calculated income. The ratio for a total monthly mortgage payment may not exceed 31% of the buyer's monthly income.

The ratios are different for other loan types and with more down payment. The ratios are designed to minimize the chances for a mortgage default and subsequent foreclosure.

The following were put in place to protect mortgage borrowers:

- Fair Debt Collection Practices Act
- Fair Credit Reporting Act
- Truth in Lending Act
- Real Estate Settlement Procedures Act
- Electronic Funds Transfers Act
- Privacy of Consumer Financial Information Act

Lenders must be competitive with interest rates and the closing costs that they charge. Disclosure is a major responsibility placed upon the lender.

What is your total house payment?

The total payment consists of principal, interest, taxes, property insurance and if required, mortgage insurance. With 20% or more down payment at the time of purchase, a conventional mortgage does not require mortgage insurance:

A monthly payment example with 20% or more down payment:

Principal & Interest	$980.00
Property Taxes	$200.00
Property Insurance	$75.00
Total PITI	**$1,255.00**

What is PITI? A mortgage company typically collects $1/12^{th}$ of the yearly property taxes and homeowner's insurance each month. The mortgage company, servicing the loan, pays the taxes and insurance when they become due. The lender guarantees the investor, who purchases the mortgage, that the property taxes and homeowner's insurance are paid and current.

Less than a 20% down payment is known as an insured conventional mortgage.

What is mortgage insurance? Mortgage insurance covers the difference between the borrower's down payment and the remaining amount up to 20%.

For example, a conventional purchase requires 5% borrower down payment. Mortgage insurance will pay the lender the remaining 15% of the sales price if the borrower defaults on the mortgage.

If you pay cash for a home, you only pay your property taxes and homeowner's insurance.

A monthly payment example with less than 20% down payment:

Principal & Interest	$980.00
Property Taxes	$200.00
Property Insurance	$75.00
Mortgage Insurance	$150.00
Total PITI	**$1,405.00**

You could label this total payment amount as PITII. (This acronym does not exist.)

FHA monthly mortgage payments also include monthly mortgage insurance in the total monthly payment. Some borrowers will increase their down payment or take out a second mortgage to avoid paying mortgage insurance. This requires the second mortgage company's underwriter approval. Check with your loan officer to see if this is an option for you.

What is earnest money?

Earnest money is a confirmation that there is a signed and accepted purchase agreement between buyer and seller. How much earnest money is typical? I recommend 1% or 2% or 3% of the sales price as optional amounts. If the offer to purchase is $400,000.00, then the earnest money could range between $4,000.00 up to $12,000.00.

Earnest money is part of the buyer's total down payment. For example, if the down payment amount is $80,000.00 and the earnest money is

$4,000.00, then the remaining down payment of $76,000.00 is due and payable at the closing.

The loan officer will typically include these figures when providing a loan disclosure with a payment amount. One of my past buyers informed me that he was going to present earnest money to the seller for the same sales price amount! He wrote an earnest money check for the offer price which was $270,000.00. The seller accepted his offer.

Occasionally with much lower priced properties, the seller will accept $500.00 or $1,000.00 earnest money. You must have at least $1.00 for the contract to be binding and accepted.

Upon the final acceptance by both buyer and seller, the earnest money is placed with the listing broker and deposited into the broker's "earnest money trust" fund. In some states the earnest money is deposited with the title company which will be preparing the documents and conducting the closing. The earnest money may be deposited with whomever the buyer and seller mutually agree where to deposit it.

There are three common ways that the earnest money may be released from a real estate company's trust fund.

1. A successful closing.

2. A cancellation of purchase agreement signed by both buyer and seller. Both agree who will receive the earnest money.

3. A judge in a court of law, declares who should get the earnest money. (With the cancellation of purchase agreement.)

Earnest money may be refunded based on contingencies found in the purchase agreement. For example, during the inspection period or during the time for review of association documents for a condo or townhome. FHA and VA loans have language written into the purchase agreements which refunds the earnest money to the buyer if they cannot get final underwriter approval for the mortgage.

CHAPTER SIX

Selecting Your Mortgage Type

Many buyers consider their payment amount versus the purchase price.

There are hundreds of different mortgage types that are available. A great loan officer works to match the homebuyer's qualifications to the best mortgage options available to them.

Your Credit Score Is Important

A buyer's credit score is an important factor for determining the mortgage program(s) they will qualify for. Their credit score will determine the mortgage interest rate that they will be able to get.

Higher credit scores result in a lower interest rate and lower credit scores cause a higher interest rate.

Mortgage companies use three major credit bureaus and use their scores to get a combined credit score.

When their credit report is obtained, some homebuyers are made aware of a lien or judgment that has been on their credit report for a long time. Liens or judgments will cause a mortgage application to be denied. Paying off this type of debt raises the overall credit scores and allows the mortgage approval process to move forward. The creditor must provide a satisfaction of judgment to the credit bureau. Sometimes this causes a one or two-month delay for mortgage approval while the credit bureaus update the judgment as being satisfied.

Employment

A two-year history of same type employment is generally acceptable to an underwriter. Occasionally a buyer will work for another employer doing the same type of work as their previous employment.

Going from a salaried position to 100% commission-based work during the last two years does not typically work well. The loan underwriter would need tax returns showing at least two years of work earning commission and enough net profit to meet the qualifying mortgage ratio requirements.

Verification of funds

The total down payment including some reserves require verification by the lender. The funds must be verified as being saved by the buyer without any of these funds being borrowed with repayment expected. Repayment of borrowed funds could cause a financial issue with the borrower being unable to make future mortgage payments. The funds need to be "seasoned" or verified as being in the buyer's bank account for several months. See your loan officer for questions.

Down Payment

Many homebuyers believe that they need 20% down payment before they will be able to purchase a home. This is not always true. Speak to a loan officer about getting pre-approved for a mortgage. Once you are pre-approved, the loan officer will be able to present you will the options for financing that will allow you to purchase. FHA loans only require a 3.5% down payment. VA loans may only require zero down payment for qualified veterans. Some conventional loans have 3.5% or 5% down payment requirements. Some first-time homebuyer programs offer down payment assistance which might provide nearly all the down payment. Check this out with your loan officer!

The age-old standard is that a lender will loan 80% of the home's appraised value and the borrower will provide the other 20% as part of the transaction. The common term for this type of mortgage is called a conventional loan.

For example:

The sales price and appraisal confirm a $200,000.00 market value.

The borrower will put $40,000.00 down. (20%) The mortgage company will loan $160,000.00 (80%)

A mortgage investor considers the down payment, credit score, verification of funds and stable employment important considerations before approving a mortgage loan for a homebuyer.

Down Payment Assistance

Some states, counties or cities will offer qualified homebuyers, down payment assistance. These programs have parameters such as income limits for the entire household and are geared for first time homebuyers or someone who has not owned a home for the last two or three years. Some require a length of time in the home before waiving re-payment and some require re-payment at the time of a future sale of the house.

Insured Mortgages

Most homebuyers do not have 20% to put into the transaction. The common term for this type of mortgage is called an insured loan.

For example:

The sales price and appraisal confirm a $200,000.00 market value.

The borrower will put $10,000.00 down. (5%)

The mortgage company will loan $190,000.00 (95%)

A mortgage insurance company will provide private mortgage insurance also known as PMI, for the $30,000.00 (15%) amount.

In the future, if the borrower would default on making payments, then the lender will foreclose and have mortgage insurance for the $30,000.00 amount. The lender may hypothetically sell the $200,000.00 house for much less in order to safely reclaim their original $160,000.00 investment.

When private mortgage insurance is required, the buyer must be approved by a second underwriter who works for the PMI Company. They will scrutinize the entire file that the lender used to approve the buyer. In rare situations the PMI underwriter will reject a component of the file and the lender must either find another PMI company to approve the loan or the buyer is notified that their file cannot be approved. Once again, **"They who have the gold make the rules."**

Types of Insured Mortgages

Fortunately, there are many loan programs available, which have mortgage insurance available.

Some common mortgage programs are:

- FHA – a government insured loan with 3.5% down payment
- VA – a government insured loan for qualified veterans with zero down payment
- Conventional loan with 20% or more down payment
- Insured Conventional loan – less than 20% down payment
- Bond programs – special rates and income limits for first time homebuyers with some offering down payment assistance

Mortgage length of term

The most funded loan is the 30-year loan, which has 360 monthly payments. It has a more affordable lower monthly payment than a

15-year loan, which has 180 monthly payments, which cause a higher monthly payment amount.

Tip: if you take out a 30-year mortgage and make one extra payment a year, your mortgage will be paid off in about 17 years!

I have not had a homebuyer take out a 40-year loan, which may give the lender the option to change the interest rate during the 480-monthly payment term.

Fixed or Adjustable Rate mortgage

When the interest rates are low most homebuyers want to take out a 30-year fixed rate mortgage because it has the lowest monthly payment. When the interest rates go up by one percent, then millions of homebuyers suddenly do not qualify for a mortgage and cannot buy a home.

Adjustable rate mortgages have a lower interest rate than a fixed rate and generally do not help the borrower qualify for more of a mortgage amount, but their initial rate and payment is lower than fixed rates offered at the same time. There are adjustable mortgages which have one, two, three, five- and ten-year periods where the initial rate stays the same. The index is a term used to identify what financial benchmark is used to determine if the mortgage rate goes up, down or stays the same.

For example, the investors will identify a neutral financial index marker and add a margin to determine the new adjusted rate. A typical margin will add two percent or more onto the index, at time of adjustment, for any interest rate adjustment. For example, if the 10-year T-Bill is 2% and the margin is 2%, then the interest rate will be 4% until the next adjustment period.

One advantage of most adjustable rate mortgages is that if you make an additional principal payment, then your lower balance is used to calculate your mortgage payment at your next payment adjustment. See your loan officer for details.

What are Points?

Mortgage rates are based on what is called a par rate. This is what the investor wants for the yield or return on the loan. A point is an upfront cost to buy down the interest rate. If for example, the par rate for a mortgage today is 4.5% and the mortgage amount is $180,000.00, then one point is $1,800.00. For example, the one point or $1,800.00, may get the buyer a lower 4.25% interest rate. The investor who is lending the borrower $180,000.00 will get the $1,800.00 at the closing table and the investor's yield will then be the same as 4.5%.

I found an old document for a transaction in 1983 with the seller paying 6% in points so that the buyer could get a 14.5% interest rate mortgage versus 16%! Points are generally associated with higher interest rates and the need to buy down the interest rate when the borrower may not qualify with a higher rate and payment.

When interest rates are exceptionally low, points used to buy down the interest rate are rarely found in a home purchase.

What are closing costs?

Closing costs include a variety of expenses which the lender charges to complete the loan from application to closing on the home. There are a variety of expenses such as the appraisal, obtaining title insurance and other expenses. Ask your loan officer for an example of your closing costs during your pre-approval process. Closing costs may be different between lenders. Some will eliminate the closing costs but charge a much higher interest rate. It is always wise to compare the rate, closing costs and monthly payment estimate before committing to work with a specific lender. After the 2008 real estate crash, sellers are limited to paying up to 3% of the buyers closing costs. Seller paid closing costs are something that are negotiated between buyer and seller. Many final sales prices include seller paid closing costs. I have witnessed upwards of 65% to 80% of transactions which include seller paid closing costs. In an unbalanced sellers-market many buyers who are cash poor, raise the sales price by 3% of the asking price if the seller will agree to pay their 3% closing costs.

For example, the thirty-year mortgage interest rate is 4% and the cost per thousand is $4.77. To raise the $300,000.00 asking price by $9,000.00 to $309,000.00 for the seller

to pay the closing costs, would be an additional $42.93 added to the buyer's monthly mortgage payment. Many buyers who do not have the $9,000.00, but are approved for the total payment, including the additional $42.93, will happily agree to this. The goal is to get the seller to also agree.

CHAPTER SEVEN
Home Inspections

Having a home inspection may save you time, money, and expensive surprises.

Many years ago, Realtors® and homebuyers believed the FHA appraiser would conduct a home inspection in addition to completing their appraisal for establishing value. There is safety checklist that an FHA appraiser will use when they are at the property, however, they do not complete an inspection.

Because of this misperception, some homeowners and attorneys brought litigation against HUD when they found problems with their homes after they closed transactions with HUD mortgages.

Consequently, HUD created a form that all buyers must sign, acknowledging the importance of a home inspection before they sign a purchase agreement.

There is usually a home inspection addendum included with written purchase agreements. The buyer pays for the home inspection. Radon, termite, and lead-based paint inspections for example, are usually additional inspections completed by specialists. Occasionally the seller will have a home inspection completed and present it to the buyer.

The buyer may research, interview, and select who they would like to complete the home inspection for them. The inspector will want payment at the time of the inspection. Real estate agents work with many home inspectors and usually may provide the names of reputable inspectors.

The home inspection period usually allows a homebuyer to cancel the purchase agreement based on their home inspection findings. Ten calendar days are usually enough time to complete the inspection and finalize any agreed upon repairs. A home inspection is critical for a buyer who has a purchase agreement on a bank owned property or a home that has been vacant for a long period of time. In many cases the water has been turned off or winterized during the cold months of the year and leaks are not evident until the water is turned on for an inspection.

Home inspections were originally designed to discover anything that was of a risk to the buyer's health and well-being. High carbon monoxide emissions coming from a rusted-out heat exchanger in the furnace is a good example.

Besides inspecting the mechanicals, roof and structure, a home inspector looks for faulty components, which could cause harm or injury to a family. For example, a ground fault interrupter that is next to the kitchen sink, should always work.

An experienced inspector will often explain to a buyer that it is difficult to find any home that is perfect and faultless.

Submitting important items for the seller to repair occurs when a buyer wants to move forward with the purchase if the seller will repair specific items. This typically occurs during an agreed upon time between the buyer and seller for completing a home inspection and mutually agreeing on any needed repairs to be made by the seller. Numerous cosmetic repair requests by the buyer may cause some sellers to not be willing to negotiate with a buyer and offer to cancel the purchase agreement.

I have also witnessed several home inspections that do not turn up any major concerns.

Radon, termite, or lead-based paint inspections will fall under the same home inspection timeframe and the results will determine if further action is required. Because of the expense and intrusive nature of a lead-based paint inspection, they are a rarity.

Homebuyers will usually request a couple of viewings of the home before they decide to write an offer. It is an emotional experience when you find a home that you want to purchase. It is sometimes difficult to remember what some features of the home look like just a few days after seeing it for the first time. Another benefit of viewing a home during the home inspection is that you get the inspector's unbiased view of the home's condition.

It is a rare exception when a homebuyer does not get a home inspected. In an extremely competitive market, some buyers have decided to not make a home inspection contingency part of their offer to purchase. Sometimes a buyer may decide that a new or newer home does not require an inspection. This is not always a good practice unless there are specific builder warranties still in effect and transferrable to a new homeowner.

Home inspectors are human beings and they may miss something. This does not happen very often. Inspectors cannot see thru walls or beneath cement floors. For example, a seller puts up a wall in the basement to hide a defect. The inspector cannot detect the defect and some buyers choose to blame their home inspector. This happens very rarely. It is almost impossible to find a "perfect" home.

Homebuyers may want to ask home inspector candidates if they are insured. Most home inspectors are not licensed or insured. It is always wise to have a home inspection.

CHAPTER EIGHT
A Home Warranty

A home warranty is designed to insure against any costly surprises for items that may need repair.

The standard home warranty protects the buyer for one year after the day of closing. Some utility companies offer warranty plans; however, they only cover the labor and not the replacement parts.

I helped Mike, a young police officer, purchase a home that was part of an estate. About six months after Mike moved in, his air conditioning unit failed. The warranty company replaced the unit because repairing it was not possible. The warranty was one of the factors, which helped Mike decide to buy the home.

Most Home Warranty Plans cost $500 to $750 with different options. The service call or deductible will be approximate $75 to $100. Divide the warranty cost into the sales price of

$250,000 and it becomes an excellent investment.

A warranty lowers the risk of having a costly repair within the first year and gives homeowners a peace of mind. Owners are comforted to know that the furnace, air conditioner, appliances, etc. are covered for one year after closing!

Most sellers are open to paying for a home warranty for the buyer. There is also an option for seller coverage for a period between the purchase agreement and the closing date.

A home warranty paid by the seller is a negotiable item between the buyer and seller. I have had transactions where the parents purchase the warranty for their children's home. I have also had buyers purchase the home warranty themselves.

Vacant homes or bank owned properties

I remember coaching my brother, to make sure a home warranty was included in the purchase agreement for the home he was purchasing in Florida. The seller was a relocation company who was not going to be held responsible for any problems immediately after the closing. Nine months later he told me that he was the proud owner of a new air conditioner, which was installed by the home warranty company. His air conditioner failed, he paid the small service fee and it was completely covered by his home warranty because they could not repair the existing unit.

A bank owned seller will always insist on the buyer signing an addendum to the purchase agreement that will hold the bank harmless after closing. This makes the home inspection and home warranty critical components of the transaction. Many buyers purchase the home warranty because most banks will not.

Sellers who are short selling a home or who are close to losing their house to foreclosure, may not have any money to repair items, and a home warranty provides a safety net for getting repairs paid for.

Before looking at homes you should consider whether you will ask the seller to pay for a home warranty and if they reject paying for it, will you?

Several years ago, I researched the list with different types of arbitrations that took place over a one-year timeframe between buyers and sellers. Combined with a home inspection and home warranty, upwards of 75% to 80% of the problems arbitrated, would have been eliminated.

CHAPTER NINE
Arbitration

Arbitration is a cost-effective way to settle a dispute.

Arbitration is an option versus a court lawsuit for all parties involved in the transaction after closing. It is binding only if everyone signs the addendum to the purchase agreement. This includes buyer, seller and all real estate agents involved in the transaction. If all parties involved in the purchase agreement agree to arbitration, then arbitration becomes a part of the purchase agreement.

If one party involved in the purchase agreement refuses to sign the arbitration addendum, arbitration is not a part of the purchase agreement.

If arbitration is available in the state that you are purchasing a home, it is important that you understand the advantages and disadvantages.

If all parties sign arbitration, a major lawsuit may not be filed since everyone agreed to use arbitration as the method to resolve a dispute or conflict after closing. The disadvantage is you cannot sue the seller because everyone agreed to use arbitration. If you file arbitration against the seller and you lose, the decision is binding and final. (An appeal may be filed.)

Some arbitration addendums to purchase agreements now have a small claims court maximum amount as the minimum amount for filing an arbitration. In Minnesota, for example, the dollar limit for small claims is $15,000.00. Any amount over $15,000.00 would be eligible for arbitration. Any claim or dispute under $15,000.00 would only be eligible for small claims court.

Arbitration or a lawsuit are not quite common with the thousands of transactions that I have participated in or have supervised as a broker. However, if a dispute arises without an agreeable solution between all parties, then a third party such as an arbitrator or judge is needed to review all the evidence presented and to decide.

When there is a dispute after closing with no resolution and arbitration is not available, then the buyer will need to hire an attorney to file a lawsuit against the seller. Most attorneys will want a $5,000 retainer and their billable hours may accumulate into the $50,000 - $70,000 range.

Arbitration will cost $1,100 to $2,000 on the average and the advantage is the low cost to arbitrate versus litigation in court. The homeowner may still hire an attorney to represent them in an arbitration filed against the seller.

The goal of arbitration is having a fair and honorable method to reach a decision in favor of one party or the other versus a much more expensive lawsuit, which may result in the same decision.

You should decide if you are going to sign arbitration before looking at homes to purchase.

Remember, buyer, seller and both real estate agents will need to sign arbitration before it becomes an option for use after closing.

CHAPTER TEN
The paperwork

A professional real estate agent, loan officer and title closer handle all the paperwork with its details.

I was recently told that some purchase agreements in California are now 600 pages or longer!

It is common in Minnesota for purchase agreements to be 40 to 50 pages. Some relocation, short sale or bank-owned purchase agreements will exceed 100 pages!

Many first-time homebuyers find themselves overwhelmed with a stack of documents when they want to make an offer to purchase a home. It is a good idea to study an example of a standard purchase agreement printed for review before looking at homes.

Initial paperwork components when selecting an agent to work with:

- Agency disclosure forms (Who is representing you.)
- Affiliated business relationships form
- Buyer contract with real estate company
- Importance of a home inspection form (HUD disclosure)
- Disclosure forms (If applicable)
  - Lead based paint
  - Radon
  - Termite Inspections
- Closing cost worksheet
- An approval letter from a lender.
- Disclosure of compensation to broker

Basic components to purchase agreement paperwork:

- Earnest money receipt
- Purchase agreement
- Arbitration addendum Type of financing addendum
- Seller contributions to closing costs
  (if applicable)
- Inspection contingency addendum
- Seller's statement of condition disclosure
- Lead based paint addendum
  (if applicable)
- Counteroffer addendum
- Home warranty application
- Miscellaneous addendums with regards to a septic system, well, and truth in housing if applicable to the transaction.

Your real estate agent will check each form to make sure that it is signed properly. It seems that every transaction has the possibility of a missing signature or initial. It is important that everyone works together to get all forms signed and dated properly.

As a homebuyer you are given copies of all the paperwork or a password to go online and access your documents.

Data privacy laws require your paperwork to be kept confidential and safe.

The good news is that you do not need to manage all the paperwork required to purchase a home. Your real estate agent usually has a team of professionals to help with all the paperwork required for securing a mortgage, title insurance and a smooth closing.

CHAPTER ELEVEN

Finding the Right Home

What home parameters will you consider in your search to find the right home?

Getting approved by a mortgage company will help a homebuyer to determine their price range. The price range helps identify the number of properties for sale in different communities.

A friend called me and asked for advice about his purchasing a home in another state. Since I was not familiar with the area, I suggested that he find out what the median sales price was for the different cities that he was considering. Once he found the median price for the community, I suggested that he stay within ten to fifteen percent, either direction of the median price, when selecting homes to look at. The median sales price is the exact middle value of all homes sold. The average sales price may be influenced by expensive new construction or lower with inexpensive condominiums. By staying near the median price, any home buyer is assured that they will typically be in a larger price range for the home sales in that community. I believe this will help with future resale.

Usually, an important criterion is the distance to drive from the home to work. This will often determine the most favorable communities within your desired commute time radius. Several homebuyers have driven from a property to their workplace during rush hour in order to determine their commute time.

In my opinion there are four types of residential real estate homes for sale with advantages and disadvantages to each:

1) Traditional residential real estate.

The advantages include:

- An owner-occupied seller to negotiate with.
- Easier communication.
- Faster decision-making.
- Quicker closing available.

- All the expensive landscaping is in.

The disadvantages include:

- The home may have some wear and tear.

2) Short sale residential real estate.

The advantages include:

- An opportunity to purchase at below-market pricing.

The disadvantages include:

- Subject to bank(s) approval.
- Delay in weeks and sometimes months for an answer.
- No contingencies allowed by you.
- Extreme flexibility required by you – may have to close quickly.

Short sale properties are usually found in economic hard times.

3) Bank owned residential real estate.

The advantages include:

- An opportunity to purchase at below market pricing.

The disadvantages include:

- Subject to bank(s) approval, which may take longer.

- No contingencies allowed by you.

- You must accept the property condition as is.

- Expect to pay for unexpected repairs after closing.

- A clean owners deed or title may not be given – instead, a limited deed may be offered instead. (Ask your title company closer for a more in-depth explanation.)

Many banks have decided to improve the condition for some of their foreclosure properties in order to get full market value.

4) New Construction residential real estate

The advantages include:

- Builder warranties are included.
- You pick your colors.
- Everything is new.

The disadvantages include:

- It may take 120 – 180 days to build the home.
- Lots of selections need to be made.
- Less finished square footage and higher prices.

Many homebuyers will eliminate two or three of these types of real estate based on the amount of time, money, or risk they are willing to take.

Your real estate agent may help you with buying a new construction home!

Many builders prefer to work with a buyer who is represented by a real estate agent. They typically have a good transaction because the real estate agent has done a lot of the preparatory work with the buyer before they visit the builder for the first time.

What resources are you using to search for homes for sale? There are many buyer-preferred websites that buyers use when searching homes for sale. There are Zillow, Trulia, Yahoo and Realtor.com websites for example. Nearly every real estate company and virtually every real estate agent have a website with search engine capabilities.

Unfortunately, some of the major websites showcase properties that have sold months ago. Several websites pull data from sources that feature incorrect data. The uninformed public typically blames the real estate broker or salesperson.

Many years ago, the real estate associations created a cooperative system for listing all

Broker listings onto one system that is accessible to its real estate membership. The most common term used is Multiple Listing Service or MLS. Most Regional Multiple Listing Services have an automatic email search program which a Realtor® may set up for new to the market listings, listings with price changes or listings that go under contract with a homebuyer. The emails may include up-to-date and accurate listing information for listings only in the homebuyer's price range.

This technology saves homebuyers lots of time searching for homes for sale on multiple Internet websites.

Communicate with your team

It is important to establish the type of communication that works best between homebuyer, real estate agent, loan officer and title closer. Sometimes the homebuyer and agent text each other while other times, email or a phone call works better.

Technology plays an important role with electronic signatures being commonly used.

Sometimes we do not physically sign a document until loan application or closing. Some bank owned listings will not allow electronic signatures and require the buyers to physically sign the purchase agreement. This technology has been slowly allowed for some transactions.

A visit to City Hall will provide public information on a specific home such as a lot plat, which a drawing of the home on the lot, including dimensions, also maps of parks and school locations.

Some homebuyers have set up a school tour with the principal in order to better understand what the district's offering is for their children.

Townhomes and Condos

Townhomes and Condominiums offer privacy, no exterior maintenance and generally carefree living. The association leadership is typically made up of owners who have been elected President, Vice President, Treasurer and Secretary. They are charged with collecting fees to pay vendors, such vendors as garbage removal, lawn care, snow removal, exterior maintenance etc. They also enforce homeowner violations of the association rules and regulations.

As part of the purchase agreement on a townhome or condominium, the homebuyer is to receive copies of the associations declaration, if any, articles of incorporation, bylaws with rules and regulations for the association, if any and any amendments or supplemental declarations with the completed common interest community resale disclosure certificate provided by the seller or seller's agent.

In most states, the buyer is required to sign a copy of the Condominium Receipt Rider as a form of documentation. If the buyer chooses to cancel the purchase agreement, it must be delivered within ten days after the receipt of all documents and current financials. Weekends and holidays are included in the ten day right of cancellation. Check with your agent regarding your specific state's length of time.

The homebuyer may choose to contact the association management company or board members with questions or concerns.

Important details to investigate:

- Verify all Restrictions/Covenants – for example, buyer's hobbies, pets, a home business, parking restrictions etc.
- Verify association fees and what the association fees include.
- Verify if the association allows rentals.
- Verify if there is an insurance fee or if the hazard insurance is included in the dues.
- Verify if personal contents insurance is needed
- Verify the amount of cash or equivalent held in reserve.

Homebuyers are required to qualify for the loan with the association dues included in the payment. Note: this reduces the qualifying price range versus single family homes which do not have a monthly association payment.

Some single-family homes have a neighborhood association with yearly dues of a fifty to two hundred dollars. The monies are usually used to maintain the neighborhood entrance monument which sometimes include watering shrubs or flowers.

Homebuyers will encounter some single-family homes with covenants and restrictions. Sean and Cathy purchased a single-family home with restrictions on the type of fence they could install for their dogs. Some neighborhoods and cities do not allow a camper to be parked in the driveway for more than 48 hours. Some ham radio operators are not allowed to install their 30 to 40-foot towers as another example.

It is important to always obtain a copy of any association documents and read them entirely because the homeowners will need to abide by the rules and regulations set forth.

Rural Property

Homes in rural settings often have a well and septic system which need to be tested to make sure they are compliant with lender, local county, or state standards. The Seller usually provides the test results to the buyer and the lender for approval.

CHAPTER TWELVE
Looking at homes

This is the fun part!

After all your hard work you are ready to look at homes that you are qualified to purchase.

Early in my career, I would show an eager buyer twelve to fifteen homes in a day. At the end of the day, neither the buyer nor myself could remember many details of the homes we looked at. I suggest a strategy to help keep things clear in your mind as you look at homes. Starting after the second home you look at; you rank the first home or the second home as your number one. After viewing the third home, you pick a new number one. It is okay to have a number two home or even a number three home. At the end of the day, you will be able to state why you like your number one home versus the others you looked at.

Another tip that I learned; only look at three homes per home search tour. This helps you keep everything you like, top of mind. I have worked with out of town buyers who were under a time crunch and we were able to look at multiple groups of three homes at a time. We took several breaks including a lunch break in between touring homes. This helps your real estate agent adapt to any new search criteria. Your agent may then select homes that better fit your needs versus wasting your time looking at homes that are not going to work for you.

Hold the screen door for your agent while they are opening the lockbox to get the front door key. It is always nice to help your agent as they attempt to get the key out of the lockbox and open the door.

During the showing of a home, it is best if everyone stays together instead of running off in different directions. This helps communicate your likes and dislikes immediately, especially if you are with another decision maker.

Look at every home in the same order. For example, you typically enter the main door to every home and view the living room first. Then view the kitchen, dining room, bedrooms, basement, garage and then backyard for example. This will help you compare other homes in a much easier fashion.

Many listings have feature sheets available. Feature sheets will sometimes list the age of the roof, furnace, air conditioner and other components of the home. Fifteen to twenty years is the life expectancy for roofs and other mechanicals found in homes.

What if you pull up to the home and you do not like how it looks? You tell your real estate agent that you do not need to see the home. I highly suggest that you get out of the car anyway and walk into the home for even as little as thirty seconds. Why? You do it for the seller who worked hard getting ready for the showing and is sitting across the street at the neighbor's house drinking coffee and watching you.

What if the seller is at home during the showing? I recommend that you greet the seller with a smile and look at the home without engaging the seller with conversation or questions. Sometimes the seller will think you really want to buy their house and they will ask their agent to pursue your agent as if you really like the home.

How do I find out why the seller is selling? This is typically not disclosed by the listing agent. If you want to find out more information, come back to the home later and knock on the neighbor's door to ask them questions about the home or seller.

Before opening any door leading to the outside of the home, check to see if it is in a locked position. If it is, lock the door after opening it and viewing what is behind the door. Many sellers will get upset if they return from your showing appointment and they find the back door unlocked.

What if the home is listed on the internet with an open house scheduled for Sunday afternoon and you want to see it? Call your agent to set up a time to meet at the home. With the listing agent's permission, you may be able to see the home during the open house. Another option is to set up a private showing before or after the open house.

What about listening devices and home security cameras watching us during the showing? This has become more prevent as smart home technology increases. We have had sellers' comment about private buyer discussions which indicated they really wanted to buy the home. This gives the buyer a major disadvantage in negotiating the price or terms with the seller. Many multiple listing services and listing contracts with

sellers have language for disclosure to the buyer of these devices before they view the

home. It is best to keep questions or comments to yourself until you are in a more private setting outside the home.

When you walk into the home you want to purchase, you will typically know that this is your home! Many buyers have told me this. Do not be nervous, instead, get ready to make an offer!

CHAPTER THIRTEEN

Writing and negotiating an offer

It is important to know if you are in a "buyer's market" or a "seller's market."

If all the homes currently for sale in a community would take seven months or more to sell without any new listings coming onto the market, then you are in a **buyer's market.** If several homes in a community have sold with an average of 10 days on the market and there are less than three month's inventories of homes for sale, then you are in a **seller's market**.

It is important to know if you are in a Buyer or Seller market when negotiating.

In a seller's market a homebuyer may encounter a multiple offer scenario. My advice is to offer full price or higher in order to beat out the other offer or offers. Many homebuyers are happy to do so when they believe that they have found the home they really want to own.

In a buyer's market a homebuyer may find homes for sale with upwards of eighty to one hundred days on the market. Because of the excessive inventory of homes for sale, buyers may have twenty to forty homes available to compare. Most multiple listing services track the list price versus sale price percentages. In a predominant buyer's market, there is typically room for negotiating price and asking for concessions, such as 3% closing costs paid by the seller.

There are many things to consider when negotiating a home, townhome, or condominium purchase. Everyone immediately thinks of an offer price. Other negotiable items to consider are:

- What date do you want to close?
- What date do you want possession?
- What appliances would you want the seller to include in the sale?
- Do you want the window coverings included?

- Do you need closing costs to be paid by the seller?
- Do you need the seller to accept your type of financing?

I have represented many homebuyers who are willing to pay nearly full price in order to get the seller to agree to pay thousands of dollars of closing costs. The monthly payment slightly increases while the buyer may keep their remaining funds in reserve. Sometimes the buyer is very qualified but is cash poor and this offers a solution.

The closing date and possession date are negotiable with some sellers wanting a quick close and some sellers wanting a closing a several months out. Flexibility will sometimes get you a lower sales price.

Some homebuyers are given advice from well-meaning parents or friends who suggest they low ball every home that they want to purchase. My advice is to research what the list price to sales price ratio is for the community. If sellers are getting 96% of their asking price and the home is on the market for 2 days, your offer of 90% asking price probably will not be accepted.

One of my selling clients was relieved to get a much higher second offer and quickly accepted it in order to reject the first buyer who made a low offer and was reluctant to negotiate. The shock and disappointment in the voice of the first buyer's agent told me that she realized they had offended and angered the seller.

We all want to save money, but you do not want to lose your dream home because you must get a "deal." Several homebuyers have told me "We have to get this home!" while we were successfully negotiating a purchase agreement with the sellers.

If you are willing to walk away from a property, then you may certainly draw a line in the sand and be prepared to move onto another home. However, when you find a home that you absolutely love, it is important to negotiate intelligently.

Presenting Your Purchase Agreement to the Seller

We have moved from real estate agents presenting purchase agreements in person to the sellers to electronic offers being emailed to listing agents and counteroffers being emailed back to the buyer's agent. It is common for negotiations over the phone to take place as well.

Some agents are suggesting a cover letter from the buyer to the seller to get an emotional connection with the buyer. I have had several buyers write an eloquent letter to the seller. Flowering plants, pets, a desire to raise a family and other commonality make the buyer "likable." This is a common practice in a seller's market, where the seller is deciding between two or more remarkably similar offers.

Most times you will get a counteroffer back from the seller's agent. It is important to respond to a counter offer as soon as possible and you never want to delay past 48 hours, or the seller may get offended.

One buyer told his agent to sit on a seller's counteroffer for a week or two. He was determined to get a "deal." When a second buyer presented an offer the first buyer wrote a new much higher offer and was distraught after he was outbid by the other buyer. The buyer was angry with everyone in the world except himself. Unfortunately, he could have easily purchased the home for a lower price if would have just kept negotiating.

You never know when a competing buyer may show up. I have witnessed homes for sale for 180 days and suddenly multiple offers are written the same day! If you really love a home, you need to act and negotiate in a timely fashion.

Negotiate by Using Options

A seller or buyer has three options when an offer is presented, or counter offered.

- The offer may be accepted as presented.
- The offer may be rejected.
- The offer may be countered.

With a counteroffer you may sometimes give the seller a couple of options for closing dates with different prices. For example, offer a lower price for their preferred closing date or a higher price for your preferred closing date. Most people respond well to options.

Sometimes a dialogue takes place between agents, (with the permission of the homebuyer) with regards to a closing date or other details. Sometimes the offer is accepted as it is written; however, this is an exception to the norm.

Sellers usually reject low-ball offers. They do not want to even discuss negotiating because they are offended or, in their opinion, the gap between asking price and the offer price are too far apart. If an asking price is not within 5% of fair market value, most buyers will not write an offer because they do not want to offend the seller.

Counteroffers are quite common, as homebuyers want to get the lowest price possible and the seller wants the highest price. Counter offers help bring a meeting of the minds between buyers and sellers.

You may be thinking, "How many counteroffers will there be?" The answer is as many as the homebuyer and seller will tolerate. After several counteroffers, someone usually will say, "This is our last offer!"

Tip: You never want to be the last to say no.

There is a final acceptance date, which is written on the purchase agreement. This date signifies that everything has been agreed upon and starts the clock ticking with any contingencies or deadlines such as completing a home inspection. Only after you have a meeting of the minds, everything has been signed or initialed and copies have been delivered, do you have a sale!

CHAPTER FOURTEEN

From Purchase to Closing

There are several hundred "touches" in every transaction, from the purchase to closing.

Once the purchase agreement has a final acceptance date it is considered "pended." Often there are inspection and financing addendums with their appropriate contingencies which must be removed.

The real estate agent distributes final copies to the loan officer and the title closer.

Title Insurance

There are two types of title insurance that are most issued in a residential transaction.

Lender's Title Insurance is mandatory with any mortgage loan and it ensures the priority of the lender's lien and protects their interest in your home.

Owner's Title Insurance is optional insurance for your interest when a question arises regarding ownership or an insured defect found on the title. (Usually when you sell the home)

Many years ago, I sold two homes just a few blocks apart and they were built by the same builder. After living in their homes for 20 years both sellers had the same title defect found on their title which was unpaid bills by the builder. One seller took out their owner's title insurance policy that they had purchased at the time of closing and the title defect was taken care of. The other seller took out the owner's title insurance form that they did not sign and pay for at the closing. It cost them several hundred dollars to get the title defect "cured" or removed from their title so that they could close.

I have recommended to every homebuyer that I have represented, to purchase owner's title insurance.

Not all owner's title insurance policies are the same.

The **ALTA 2006 OWNER'S TITLE POLICY (Standard)** with 10 covered risks is commonly issued with the purchase of a bank-owned home.

The **ALTA 2013 HOMEOWNER'S TITLE POLICY (Enhanced)** has 32 covered risks. This ALTA enhanced title insurance policy is available for qualifying residential homes.

Do you have an insurance agent who will issue a homeowner's insurance binder for your home prior to closing? This is a mandatory requirement by the mortgage company. It is the same if you have an auto loan. You must have the auto insured and name the bank as insured on the policy. The mortgage company requires their financial interests in your home to be insured in case of a fire and the home is a total loss. So, will you! You will need an insurance binder issued to start on the day of closing. You may use your current insurance agent or ask your real estate agent for an insurance agent referral. The insurance binder must be delivered to the loan officer prior to closing or brought with you to the closing.

It is common to have a courtesy walk-through within five days before closing. The home is usually in an uproar with boxes and personal items ready for a moving truck. But this walk-through allows the buyer to make sure the home is intact and any personal property such as appliances or draperies are left in the home. Rarely will a seller take items that were included in the purchase agreement. A walk-through is an opportunity to run the furnace, turn on the oven and dishwasher for example. If something is not quite right, there is some time before closing for the seller to make it right.

Sometimes after closing, the seller will give the homebuyer a guided tour of the home and show them some maintenance tips such as how to change the air filter in the furnace. This tour may happen before the closing or not at all.

Here is a list of things that will happen through closing:

- Your loan officer may get requests from the mortgage underwriter for more documentation.

- The appraiser will set up an appointment to assess the home, complete an appraisal and send it to the mortgage company.
- Title work is ordered, and clear title allows for a title insurance policy to be issued.
- The mortgage and owner's policies are to be part of the settlement.
- Contact an insurance agent and obtain a binder for a one-year homeowner's policy for the home. Deliver a copy to your title closer.
- Seven to ten days before closing, you will want to set up the utilities in your name effect the day of closing.
- Your loan officer and processor will submit your loan file for final underwriting when they have obtained your credit, employment, assets, debts, title work and appraisal.
- With a minimum of three days' notice your loan officer will send you the final amount needed to close, including any fixed broker commission. You will need to obtain a cashier's check made out to the title company.

- The title company will send you a letter with the date, time, address, and contact information for the closing. The closing is held at the buyer's title company.
- You may close in the same room with the sellers or you may not. Some sellers will not be able to attend the closing and sign their documents a day or two earlier.
- There is new technology trend for signing most of your documents online, within 24 hours of your actual closing time.
- Your property taxes and homeowner's insurance will be escrowed with each monthly mortgage payment. Unless you are paying cash. Then you are responsible for making those payments.
- Depending on the state you are purchasing in, there may be homesteading or other ownership responsibilities right after the closing.
- Your real estate agent will be in contact with your mortgage and title company

CHAPTER FIFTEEN

The Closing

The closing is meant for a time of signing documents and transfer of ownership.

About a week to ten days before closing, contact all utility companies and city service providers in order to have meters read and to transfer them into your name starting on the date of your closing.

The closing requires a homebuyer to bring the following:

- Your valid driver's license with photo ID - it will be photocopied by your closer.

- A cashier's check made out to yourself and the title company that you are closing with.

- A record of addresses where you have lived for the last 10 years.

The closing is a time to sign a large stack of mortgage papers and other necessary documents. These are standard documents and the lender will not allow them to be changed. Your closer will explain the documents, figures and the escrow account which will be set up for the payment of property taxes and homeowner's insurance.

The HUD-1 statement will list your closing costs along with any other charges and credits. After signing the paperwork your closer will make copies of all documents for your file. Your last duty is to sign your cashier's check over to the title company.

If the seller(s) attends the closing, he/she will usually give you keys, garage door openers, appliance manuals, etc.

It is a good idea to exchange phone numbers with the seller in case you have questions about the home after closing or if you receive a package mistakenly delivered to you.

CHAPTER SIXTEEN

How does your agent get paid?

Most listing brokers have a compensation agreement to pay a buyer's broker commission.

When buyer representation first appeared many years ago, the buyer paid a buyer broker commission to represent them in the purchase of a home.

This caused conflict with many listing agreements because the seller's broker had already agreed to pay an agent who brought a buyer's purchase agreement to a successful closing. The buyer's broker often negotiated a lower price and would not accept payment from the listing broker and vice versus. The buyer was required to pay the commission owed at closing or increase the mortgage amount they were borrowing if they did not have the funds.

In most multiple listing service transactions, the seller's broker pays the buyer's broker. Before the homebuyer signs a purchase agreement, they sign a disclosure that states the listing broker is paying   commission owed by the buyer to the broker representing them. This disclosure notifies the buyer that they will not be liable for paying the buyer broker's commission. However, they will still owe a fixed commission.

Fixed commissions

What is a fixed commission? Real estate companies get paid a commission along with an additional fixed commission for every transaction. The commission paid will vary depending on the amount that the listing broker along with the seller, decide to pay the buyer's broker. The additional fixed commission is like paying a baggage fee for your airline flight.

The fixed commission may be $499.00 for example, with some companies charging less and some more. The buyer and seller pay the same fixed commission. The real estate company keeps the fixed commission and the remaining commission is split between the real estate company and the salesperson. The buyer pays their owed fixed commission at closing.

Commission is included in the sales price and the fixed commission is paid out of pocket at closing.

CHAPTER SEVENTEEN

After Closing

Your tax preparer may need to review the HUD-1 documents from your closing.

When the homebuyer takes possession of their home in Minnesota, they need to file for homestead classification at the City Hall or the county courthouse. (Not all states have homesteading.)

Most real estate companies have web-based storage with access to all the transaction documents including the HUD-1 statement. This is very convenient during tax time when your accountant may want to review it for any eligible tax deductions.

The National Association of Realtors has and will continue to fight for mortgage interest and property tax deductions for all homeowners.

The end of this book contains a checklist that I developed that you may use to begin the homebuying process. My goal is for you to save valuable time and money while purchasing your home. Have a smooth closing!

AFTERWORD

Together we are making a difference in our world with a percentage of ASKWYNHOW.COM profits donated to helping others who lack housing, water, or food. My wife and I, and several friends, support clean water efforts in Ethiopia. I also support organizations that support families with housing needs and children who do not have enough to eat.

I pray that your home buying experience is pleasant and that you are blessed by the outcome. Please feel free to give this book a 5-star rating on Amazon. I appreciate you taking the time to do this!

We Create Success Together!

Home Buying Checklist

- ☐ Select your real estate agent to represent you.

- ☐ Sign an exclusive right to represent buyer contract.

- ☐ Select the type of financing program best suited for you.

- ☐ Obtain a closing costs worksheet and an estimate of the down payment requirements

- ☐ Get approved for your mortgage.

- ☐ Determine if you need or want the seller to contribute to paying closing costs?

- ☐ Decide if you want to purchase a single family, townhome, condo or new construction?

- ☐ Determine the approximate price range that you want to purchase.

- [ ] Determine the communities you want to live in.

- [ ] Do you want to have a home inspection contingency?

- [ ] Do you want to have a radon test or other inspections?

- [ ] Do you want a home warranty included in the sale?

- [ ] What date do you want to close?

- [ ] What appliances would you need the seller to include in the sale?

- [ ] Do you want to sign the arbitration addendum?

- [ ] Do you want to purchase an owner's title insurance policy?

- [ ] Do you have an insurance agent who will issue a homeowner's insurance binder prior to closing?

☐ Are you able to obtain a cashier's check for the remaining down payment and closing costs?

Wyn Ray Credentials

- Minneapolis Area Association of Realtors – 2018 Heart of the Community Award, recognizing REALTORS® who give back.
- NAR Magazine's 2016 Good Neighbor Award - REALTOR® Magazine's Good Neighbor Awards recognize REALTORS® who have made an extraordinary impact on their community, or on the national or world stage, through volunteer work.
- Graduate of Realtors Institute – *A Minnesota Association of Realtors Designation*
- Certified Residential Specialist – *A National Association of Realtors Designation*
- Certified Residential Broker –*A National Association of Realtors Designation*

- Senior Residential Advisor - *A Minnesota Association of Realtors Designation*
- Certified Distressed Property Expert – *Charfin Institute*
- Certified Probate Specialist - *J G Banks Institute*
- Integrity Selling Specialist - *Certified by Integrity Solutions*
- Integrity Coaching Specialist - *Certified by Integrity Solutions*
- ePro (Technology) - *A National Association of Realtors Designation*
- Accredited Buyer's Representative - A *National Association of Realtors Designation*
- Wrote and Instructed three courses for Minnesota Real Estate Continuing Education - *Approved by The Minnesota Department of Commerce*
- Author of *Selling Probate Property*
- Author of *Easy 5-Step House Selling Guide*
- Author of *A Step by Step Home Buying Guide*

Wyn Ray is currently a licensed Real Estate Broker in the State of Minnesota. #20399255.

www.ingramcontent.com/pod-product-compliance
Lightning Source LLC
Chambersburg PA
CBHW060507280326
41933CB00014B/2889